ASOGWA JUSTINA

The Conceptual Revolution: Shaping the Future with Ideas

Copyright © 2024 by Asogwa Justina

All rights reserved. No part of this publication may be reproduced, stored or transmitted in any form or by any means, electronic, mechanical, photocopying, recording, scanning, or otherwise without written permission from the publisher. It is illegal to copy this book, post it to a website, or distribute it by any other means without permission.

Asogwa Justina asserts the moral right to be identified as the author of this work.

Asogwa Justina has no responsibility for the persistence or accuracy of URLs for external or third-party Internet Websites referred to in this publication and does not guarantee that any content on such Websites is, or will remain, accurate or appropriate.

First edition

This book was professionally typeset on Reedsy.
Find out more at reedsy.com

Contents

1	The Catalyst	1
2	The First Threat	5
3	Unlikely Allies	9
4	The Lab Break-In	14
5	The Rival Innovator	18
6	The Corporate Spy	23
7	The Prototype	28
8	The Government's Interest	34
9	The Global Pursuit	39
10	The Betrayal	44
11	The Final Showdown	49
12	The New Dawn	55

1

The Catalyst

Rain lashed against the windows of Dr. Ethan Cole's small laboratory, a relentless drumbeat that mirrored his pounding heart. He stood over his workbench, the dim light of a single lamp illuminating the chaotic array of sketches, blueprints, and prototypes scattered before him. His eyes, bloodshot from countless sleepless nights, were fixed on a device no larger than a smartphone. The Catalyst, as he had come to call it, was a marvel of engineering and innovation—a device that could revolutionize energy consumption and transform society.

Ethan adjusted his glasses, his fingers trembling with anticipation as he made the final connection. The Catalyst hummed to life, its core emitting a soft, blue glow. He held his breath, watching the readings on his monitor. The numbers spiked, then stabilized, indicating a successful activation. A smile crept across his face. After years of labor, countless failures, and near financial ruin, he had done it. The Catalyst was real, and it worked.

Suddenly, a loud crash shattered the moment. Ethan's head snapped up, his heart skipping a beat. He glanced at the door, which now hung ajar, a gust of wind whipping through the gap. Cautiously, he moved towards it, every step echoing in the silent room. He peered into the hallway, his eyes scanning for any sign of intruders. Nothing. He closed the door, securing the lock, and returned to his workbench.

As he resumed his seat, Ethan couldn't shake the feeling of being watched. He dismissed it as paranoia—after all, he had been under immense stress. But as he leaned back in his chair, a shadow flitted across the room, barely visible in the periphery of his vision. He whipped around, but the lab was empty.

Ethan's phone buzzed, startling him. He picked it up, expecting a call from his partner, Claire, who had been out of town. Instead, the screen displayed an unknown number. Hesitant, he answered.

"Dr. Cole," a distorted voice crackled through the speaker, "you need to stop."

"Who is this?" Ethan demanded, his pulse quickening.

"That device... the Catalyst. It's dangerous. You have no idea what you're dealing with."

Ethan's grip tightened on the phone. "Who are you? How do you know about the Catalyst?"

"That's not important," the voice replied. "What's important is that you destroy it. Now."

Before Ethan could respond, the line went dead. He stared at the phone, his mind racing. Who could know about the Catalyst? He had been so careful, so secretive. The possibilities churned in his head, none of them comforting.

Determined to protect his work, Ethan decided to increase security. He transferred all his data to an encrypted drive and locked the Catalyst in a reinforced safe. As he secured the lab, a sense of unease settled over him. He couldn't shake the feeling that he was being watched, hunted.

That night, sleep eluded him. He lay in bed, staring at the ceiling, the events of the day replaying in his mind. The crash, the shadow, the phone call—it all felt like the opening moves in a sinister game. Who could want to stop his research? Rivals? Corporate spies? The government? Each theory seemed as plausible as the last.

Morning came, and with it, a renewed sense of determination. Ethan arrived at the lab early, his mind set on pushing forward despite the threats. As he worked, the rain outside intensified, the storm growing fiercer. He was in the middle of fine-tuning the Catalyst when a loud banging echoed through the building.

Ethan froze, his heart thudding in his chest. The sound came again, more insistent. He edged towards the door, grabbing a metal rod for protection. He reached the door and peered through the peephole, his breath hitching. Two men in dark suits stood outside, their expressions stern and unyielding.

"Dr. Cole," one of them called, "we need to speak with you."

Ethan's grip on the rod tightened. "Who are you?"

"We're with the Department of Energy. It's imperative that we discuss your research."

Ethan hesitated. Government involvement was one of his worst fears, but there was no avoiding it now. He unlocked the door and opened it cautiously.

"May we come in?" the second man asked, his voice calm but firm.

Ethan nodded, stepping aside. The men entered, their eyes immediately sweeping the room, taking in every detail.

"We've been monitoring your progress, Dr. Cole," the first man began. "Your work on the Catalyst has drawn significant attention."

"Monitoring? What right do you have?" Ethan's voice shook with a mix of anger and fear.

"National security," the man replied simply. "The Catalyst represents a breakthrough that could change the global energy landscape. It also poses a substantial risk if misused."

Ethan's mind raced. National security? Risks? He had envisioned the Catalyst as a force for good, a way to end energy crises and reduce environmental impact. But these men saw it as something else—something dangerous.

"We need you to hand over all your research," the second man said, his tone brooking no argument. "For your safety and the safety of others."

Ethan's instincts screamed at him to refuse, to protect his creation. But the cold, hard reality of the situation settled over him. He was one man against an unseen force much larger and more powerful than he could comprehend.

"I need time," Ethan said, trying to buy a moment to think. "This isn't something I can just hand over."

"We understand," the first man said. "But know this, Dr. Cole—time is running out. For all of us."

With that ominous warning, they left, leaving Ethan standing in the middle of his lab, his mind a whirlpool of fear and determination. The Catalyst was more than just an idea now; it was a beacon, drawing attention from every corner, and the revolution it promised had already begun to shape the future, whether he was ready or not.

2

The First Threat

The wind howled outside, battering against the windows of Ethan's small apartment. He sat hunched over his laptop at the kitchen table, the glow from the screen casting sharp shadows across his face. Files upon files of encrypted data scrolled past as he tried to make sense of the day's events. The meeting with the government agents had left him rattled, but he knew he couldn't let fear paralyze him. He had to understand what he was dealing with and how to protect his work.

A sharp knock on the door interrupted his thoughts. Ethan's heart skipped a beat. He wasn't expecting anyone. He stood up slowly, the chair scraping loudly against the tile floor, and moved towards the door. He peered through the peephole but saw no one. Warily, he opened the door just enough to glance outside. The hallway was empty, but as he looked down, he noticed a small, unmarked envelope lying on the doormat.

Ethan picked it up, his fingers tingling with a mix of curiosity and dread. He closed the door and walked back to the kitchen table, tearing the envelope open with trembling hands. Inside was a single piece of paper with a typed message:

Stop your work on the Catalyst. This is your only warning.

No signature, no indication of who it might be from. Ethan's mind raced. Who could have sent this? The government agents? A rival scientist? Or someone else entirely? He crumpled the note in frustration, tossing it into the trash. But the sense of unease lingered, gnawing at him.

He sat back down and forced himself to focus. He had to fortify his security measures. Pulling up the encryption protocols, he spent the next few hours reinforcing his digital defenses, setting up firewalls and backup systems. As he worked, his phone buzzed with a text message. He glanced at the screen:

Unknown Number: This is not a game, Dr. Cole. Stop now, or you'll regret it.

Ethan's blood ran cold. Another threat, more direct this time. He couldn't ignore it any longer. He needed help. But who could he trust? The government agents seemed too dangerous, and his colleagues were potential rivals. Then, he remembered the hacker who had contacted him before. An unlikely ally, but perhaps his only hope.

Ethan quickly typed out an email to the anonymous address he had for the hacker, explaining the situation and requesting urgent assistance. He hit send and leaned back, exhaling slowly. Now, he could only wait and hope for a response.

Hours passed. The storm outside grew more violent, and the power flickered once or twice, plunging the apartment into darkness before the lights came back on. Ethan kept working, his nerves frayed but his determination unbroken. Just as dawn was breaking, his laptop pinged with a new message. It was from the hacker.

Subject: Re: Urgent Assistance Needed

THE FIRST THREAT

Message:

Dr. Cole,

I received your message. The threats you mentioned are serious. We need to act fast. I've traced the origin of the threats to a highly sophisticated network, possibly linked to a corporate entity or a rogue government faction.

I'll help you fortify your systems and track down the source. But you need to be ready for anything. This is a dangerous game we're playing.

Stay vigilant. I'll be in touch with more instructions soon.

- Cipher

Relief washed over Ethan, mingled with a fresh wave of anxiety. At least he wasn't alone in this anymore. But the stakes had just been raised. He couldn't afford any mistakes.

Over the next few days, Ethan and Cipher worked in tandem, securing Ethan's research and setting up traps to catch any digital intruders. The process was grueling, with Ethan constantly looking over his shoulder, expecting another threat to materialize at any moment.

One night, as he was packing up to leave the lab, Ethan noticed a black SUV parked across the street, its windows tinted so dark he couldn't see inside. His stomach tightened. He had seen the same vehicle a few times now, always parked nearby, always watching. He hurried back inside and called Cipher, explaining the situation.

"You're being tailed," Cipher said bluntly. "It's time to relocate your research. They know where you are."

Ethan's mind raced. Relocate? Where could he possibly go? But there was no other option. He gathered his most crucial files, loaded them onto an encrypted drive, and stuffed it into his bag. He grabbed the Catalyst from its secure case and carefully placed it in a protective pouch.

As he was about to leave, his phone buzzed with another message from the unknown number:

Last chance, Dr. Cole. Stop now, or face the consequences.

Ethan's breath hitched. He glanced around the lab one last time, then bolted out the back door, slipping into the shadows of the alleyway. He moved quickly, ducking through side streets and alleys, his heart pounding in his chest. He didn't stop until he reached a small, nondescript motel on the edge of town. Checking in under a false name, he secured his room and double-locked the door.

Ethan sat on the edge of the bed, clutching the Catalyst. He knew he was in deeper than he had ever imagined. The threats were real, and whoever was behind them was serious. But he couldn't stop now. The Catalyst was too important. It had the power to change the world, and he wouldn't let fear or intimidation stand in his way.

As he settled in for another sleepless night, Ethan couldn't help but wonder: Who were his enemies, and how far were they willing to go to stop him? The answers eluded him, but one thing was clear—he had to stay one step ahead, no matter the cost.

3

Unlikely Allies

Ethan's new temporary home was a cramped, dingy room with peeling wallpaper and a single flickering light bulb. He barely noticed the squalor, his mind consumed by the dangers lurking outside. Sleep had become a luxury he could no longer afford. He paced the room, the Catalyst always within arm's reach, its presence both a comfort and a curse. His phone buzzed, drawing his attention away from the paranoia that gnawed at his thoughts.

The message was from Cipher: **"Meet me at the old warehouse on Dock Street. Midnight. Come alone."**

Ethan hesitated, the weight of the decision pressing down on him. Cipher had been helpful, but could he trust someone he had never met? The threats were escalating, and time was running out. He couldn't afford to be cautious any longer. He packed his laptop, the Catalyst, and a few essential tools, then slipped out of the motel under the cover of darkness.

The streets were eerily quiet as he made his way to Dock Street. The warehouse loomed ahead, a hulking shadow against the night sky. Its broken windows and rusted exterior gave it an abandoned look, but Ethan knew better. He approached cautiously, every sense on high alert.

A figure emerged from the shadows, clad in a dark hoodie, face obscured by the dim light. Ethan's pulse quickened. He tightened his grip on the bag containing the Catalyst, ready to run if necessary.

"Dr. Cole," the figure called out, their voice familiar from the phone calls. "I'm Cipher."

Ethan took a tentative step forward. "How do I know I can trust you?"

"You don't," Cipher replied, pulling back the hood to reveal a young woman with sharp, intelligent eyes. "But right now, I'm your best shot at staying alive and keeping your research safe."

The two stared at each other, a silent understanding passing between them. Ethan nodded slowly. "Alright. Let's do this."

Cipher led him inside the warehouse, weaving through a maze of old crates and machinery until they reached a small, makeshift office. It was cluttered with computer equipment, cables snaking across the floor like vines. Cipher gestured for Ethan to sit, then pulled up a chair opposite him.

"We don't have much time," she said, her fingers flying over the keyboard as she brought up a series of complex data streams. "I've traced the threats to a shell corporation. They're good—real good. But I found a lead."

Ethan leaned in, his eyes scanning the screen. "Who are they?"

"Best guess? A rogue faction within a major tech conglomerate," Cipher explained. "They see the Catalyst as a threat to their control over the energy market. If your invention goes public, it could disrupt everything."

Ethan's mind reeled. "So, what do we do?"

Cipher glanced at him, a determined glint in her eyes. "We hit back. I've set up a honey pot to lure them in. When they take the bait, we'll trace them back to their source. But it means you'll have to expose your research again, at least temporarily."

Ethan's stomach churned. He had worked so hard to protect the Catalyst, but now he had to risk it all. He took a deep breath, steeling himself. "Let's do it."

For the next few hours, they worked together, uploading a decoy version of the Catalyst's data to a secure server. Cipher's fingers flew across the keyboard, her focus unbroken. Ethan marveled at her skill, realizing just how much he needed her expertise.

As the clock ticked towards midnight, a sense of dread settled over him. They were walking into a trap of their own making, hoping to catch their enemies unaware. Every sound outside the warehouse seemed amplified, each creak and groan a potential threat.

Suddenly, Cipher's computer beeped. "They're in," she said, her voice tense with anticipation. "They're trying to download the data."

Ethan watched as lines of code streamed across the screen, Cipher's program tracing the digital fingerprints back to their source. The minutes stretched into an eternity, the tension in the room palpable.

"Got it!" Cipher exclaimed, a triumphant smile breaking through her usual stoicism. "We have their location."

Ethan leaned closer, his eyes widening as he read the coordinates. "That's... that's the headquarters of Titan Technologies."

Cipher nodded. "Looks like our suspicions were right. Now we need proof, something concrete to bring them down."

Ethan's mind raced. "I have an old colleague who works there. He might be able to help us from the inside."

"Good," Cipher replied. "We'll need all the help we can get. But be careful. If they suspect anything, your colleague could be in serious danger."

Ethan nodded, determination hardening his resolve. "I'll reach out to him. We can't let them win."

As they finalized their plans, a loud crash echoed through the warehouse. Both Ethan and Cipher froze, their eyes locking in silent alarm. Footsteps echoed in the distance, drawing closer with each passing second.

"Hide," Cipher hissed, grabbing her laptop and shoving it into a bag. "Now!"

Ethan ducked behind a stack of crates, his heart pounding in his chest. He could see Cipher doing the same on the other side of the room. The footsteps grew louder, more deliberate, until they stopped just outside the makeshift office.

The door creaked open, and a beam of light swept across the room. Ethan held his breath, willing himself to remain still. The light passed over him, then moved on. He heard muffled voices, the words indistinct but the tone menacing.

After what felt like an eternity, the footsteps retreated, and the door closed with a soft click. Ethan waited a few moments longer, then slowly emerged from his hiding place. Cipher did the same, her face pale but composed.

"That was too close," she whispered. "We need to move. Now."

They gathered their things quickly, slipping out of the warehouse and into the night. As they made their way to a safer location, Ethan couldn't help but feel a glimmer of hope. They had found an ally in Cipher, and together, they might just have a chance to uncover the truth and protect the Catalyst.

But the danger was far from over. And as the shadows closed in around them, Ethan knew that the real battle was only just beginning.

4

The Lab Break-In

Ethan's hands shook as he inserted the key into the lock of his lab. The drive to the university had been nerve-wracking; every car that followed him too closely felt like a threat, every pedestrian a potential spy. He stepped inside the lab and closed the door behind him, taking a moment to breathe in the familiar scent of chemicals and metal. It was supposed to be a sanctuary, but tonight it felt like a trap.

He turned on the lights, illuminating the cluttered space. Equipment and prototypes littered every surface, and the Catalyst, now safely locked away in a reinforced cabinet, seemed to hum with a life of its own. He walked over to his computer and logged in, his mind focused on the task ahead. He needed to contact his colleague at Titan Technologies and figure out a way to expose the corporate conspiracy.

Just as he started composing an encrypted message, a loud crash echoed through the building. Ethan froze, his heart racing. He listened, straining to catch any sound over the pounding of his heart. Another crash, closer this time. Someone was breaking in.

Ethan grabbed the nearest heavy object—a wrench—and crept towards the door. He peered through the small glass window, his blood running cold at the sight of two masked figures moving methodically through the hallway. They were dressed in black, their movements precise and coordinated. These were no common thieves; they were professionals.

He retreated back into the lab, his mind racing. He needed to hide the Catalyst. He opened the reinforced cabinet and grabbed the device, wrapping it in a protective cloth. Glancing around, he spotted a vent cover near the floor. He quickly unscrewed it and placed the Catalyst inside, replacing the cover just as the door to the lab burst open.

Ethan ducked behind a large piece of machinery, holding his breath as the intruders entered. They moved with military precision, sweeping their flashlights across the room. One of them spoke into a radio, the words too muffled for Ethan to hear. They split up, one moving towards the computers, the other searching through the equipment.

Ethan's mind raced. He needed to get out, but any movement might give him away. He watched as the intruder at the computers inserted a USB drive and began downloading data. The other was methodically searching the room, drawing closer to Ethan's hiding spot.

Suddenly, the sound of footsteps echoed from the hallway. The intruders froze, their heads snapping towards the door. Ethan took the opportunity to move, crawling silently towards the opposite end of the lab. He reached another piece of machinery and crouched behind it, praying he hadn't been seen.

The footsteps grew louder, and then a new figure appeared in the doorway. Ethan's eyes widened in shock. It was Claire, his partner, who had been out of town. She stepped into the lab, her eyes widening as she took in the scene.

"What the hell is going on here?" she demanded, her voice trembling with anger and fear.

The intruders didn't respond. Instead, they advanced towards her, their intentions clear. Claire backed up, her hands raised defensively.

"Wait! You don't have to do this," she pleaded, but her words fell on deaf ears.

Ethan couldn't stand by and watch. He grabbed the wrench and stood up, stepping out from his hiding place. "Leave her alone!"

The intruders turned, surprise flickering in their eyes. Ethan took advantage of the momentary distraction and charged, swinging the wrench with all his might. He struck the nearest intruder on the arm, causing him to drop his flashlight with a grunt of pain.

"Run, Claire!" Ethan shouted, turning to face the second intruder. Claire hesitated for a moment, then bolted towards the door.

The second intruder lunged at Ethan, but he was ready. He dodged the attack and swung the wrench again, this time connecting with the intruder's leg. The man stumbled, giving Ethan enough time to grab a nearby chair and hurl it at the computers. The monitor shattered, sparks flying as the USB drive was knocked loose.

The first intruder recovered and charged at Ethan, tackling him to the ground. Ethan struggled, but the intruder was stronger, pinning him down with ease. The second intruder picked up the USB drive and slipped it into his pocket, then nodded to his partner.

"Let's go," he said, his voice cold and emotionless.

The first intruder released Ethan and stood up, kicking him hard in the ribs for good measure. Pain exploded in Ethan's side, but he forced himself to his feet as the intruders made their escape. Claire rushed back into the room, her face pale with fear.

"Ethan, are you okay?" she asked, helping him to a chair.

"I'm fine," he gasped, clutching his side. "They took something—data. We have to stop them."

Claire nodded, her expression determined. "I saw them get into a black SUV. I'll call the police."

Ethan shook his head. "No. They're professionals. By the time the police get here, they'll be long gone. We need to follow them."

Claire hesitated, then nodded. "Okay. Let's go."

Ethan grabbed the Catalyst from its hiding place and stuffed it into his bag. Together, they raced out of the lab and into the night, determined to reclaim what had been stolen and uncover the truth behind the conspiracy. The chase had only just begun, and Ethan knew that the stakes had never been higher.

5

The Rival Innovator

Ethan and Claire sped through the rain-soaked streets, the wipers of Claire's car struggling to keep up with the downpour. The black SUV they were tailing was a few cars ahead, its taillights barely visible through the torrent. Ethan clutched the Catalyst protectively in his lap, the weight of the night's events pressing heavily on his shoulders.

"We're getting too close," Claire muttered, her knuckles white on the steering wheel.

"Keep distance, but don't lose them," Ethan replied, his eyes never leaving the SUV. The thought of what was at stake drove him forward, despite the danger.

The SUV suddenly veered off the main road, taking a sharp turn onto a side street. Claire followed, the car skidding slightly on the wet pavement. They found themselves in an industrial area, the buildings looming dark and foreboding against the night sky.

The SUV pulled into a large warehouse, its doors sliding shut behind it. Claire parked a safe distance away, and they watched as the intruders disappeared inside.

"Now what?" Claire asked, her voice tense.

"We need to get in there," Ethan said, his mind racing. "But we can't just walk through the front door."

Claire nodded, scanning the perimeter. "There," she pointed to a side entrance partially obscured by stacks of pallets.

They exited the car and crept towards the entrance, the rain masking their footsteps. The door was locked, but Claire produced a set of lock-picking tools from her bag. Ethan raised an eyebrow.

"I learned a few things in my old job," she whispered with a smirk, deftly unlocking the door.

Inside, the warehouse was dimly lit, filled with rows of machinery and stacked crates. The sound of voices echoed from a nearby room. Ethan and Claire moved silently, sticking to the shadows.

They reached a large, open space where the SUV was parked. The two intruders were standing with another figure—a man in his early thirties, dressed in a sleek, tailored suit. His presence radiated authority and arrogance. Ethan's breath caught in his throat as he recognized the man: Marcus Holloway, a rival innovator known for his ruthless tactics and cutting-edge technology.

"So, did you get it?" Marcus asked, his tone impatient.

The intruder with the USB drive nodded and handed it over. Marcus plugged it into a laptop, his eyes lighting up as the data appeared on the screen.

"This is it," he murmured. "The Catalyst."

Ethan clenched his fists, anger bubbling within him. Marcus had always been one step ahead, always willing to cut corners and betray trust to achieve his goals. Now, he had his hands on Ethan's most important work.

Claire placed a hand on Ethan's arm, grounding him. They needed a plan, and they needed it fast.

Marcus continued to speak, his voice carrying through the warehouse. "With this, Titan Technologies will be unstoppable. We can corner the market on energy, and no one will be able to challenge us."

Ethan's mind raced. He needed to get the Catalyst back and expose Marcus's scheme. But how? As they watched, a new idea formed in his mind. It was risky, but it might just work.

He whispered his plan to Claire, who nodded in agreement. They moved back into the shadows, carefully making their way to a control panel on the wall. Ethan's fingers flew over the buttons, shutting off the lights and plunging the warehouse into darkness.

Shouts of confusion erupted from Marcus and his men. Ethan and Claire moved quickly, using the cover of darkness to their advantage. They reached Marcus's laptop, and Claire yanked the USB drive free while Ethan grabbed the laptop itself.

"Who's there?" Marcus's voice was sharp, filled with anger and fear.

Ethan didn't answer. He and Claire sprinted towards the exit, their footsteps echoing in the cavernous space. A flashlight beam cut through the darkness behind them, followed by the sound of running feet.

They burst through the side door and into the rain, not stopping until they reached Claire's car. They jumped in, and Claire started the engine, tires squealing as they sped away.

"Did you get it?" Ethan asked, breathless.

Claire held up the USB drive, a triumphant smile on her face. "Got it."

Ethan's relief was short-lived as he glanced in the rearview mirror. The black SUV was back, its headlights glaring through the rain. "They're following us."

Claire's expression hardened. "Hold on."

She pushed the car to its limits, weaving through the streets in a desperate bid to lose their pursuers. The SUV stayed close, its driver matching her every move. Ethan clutched the laptop and the Catalyst, his mind racing for a solution.

"Take the next left," he instructed, his voice steady despite the fear coursing through him.

Claire complied, the car skidding around the corner. They found themselves on a narrow, winding road, the SUV still on their tail. Ahead, Ethan spotted an alleyway barely wide enough for their car.

"Go through there," he urged.

Claire hesitated for a fraction of a second, then veered into the alleyway. The SUV tried to follow but got stuck, its sides scraping against the brick walls. Ethan and Claire sped out the other side and into the open road.

"We did it," Claire breathed, glancing at Ethan.

"For now," he replied, his mind already on the next step. "We need to get this data to the authorities. Marcus won't stop until he gets what he wants."

They drove in silence, the rain gradually easing up. The weight of the night's events settled over them, but they knew there was no time to rest. The battle was far from over, and the stakes were higher than ever.

As they pulled into the parking lot of a nearby safe house, Ethan felt a renewed sense of determination. They had the Catalyst, and they had the evidence. Now, they just needed to find a way to use it. With Claire by his side, he felt a glimmer of hope. Together, they would expose Marcus and ensure that the Catalyst's potential was used for the greater good, not for the greed of a single corporation.

But as they stepped out of the car, a figure emerged from the shadows, a gun pointed directly at them. Ethan's heart sank as he recognized the face—one of Marcus's men.

"Give me the Catalyst," the man demanded, his voice cold and unwavering.

Ethan and Claire exchanged a glance, their minds racing. The night's dangers were far from over, and they were about to face their biggest challenge yet.

6

The Corporate Spy

Ethan and Claire stood frozen, the glint of the gun reflecting the dim streetlight. The man stepped closer, his grip on the weapon steady, his eyes cold. Ethan's mind raced, searching for a way out. The Catalyst and the USB drive were too valuable to surrender, but one wrong move could mean their lives.

"Hand it over," the man repeated, his voice low and threatening.

Claire glanced at Ethan, her eyes conveying a silent message: stall for time. Ethan took a deep breath, trying to steady his nerves.

"Look, we don't want any trouble," Ethan said, his voice calm despite the fear bubbling inside him. "Let's talk about this."

The man sneered. "There's nothing to talk about. Give me the Catalyst, or you both die."

Ethan's heart pounded, but he forced himself to stay calm. He shifted slightly, trying to obscure the laptop and the USB drive from the man's view. Claire subtly moved her hand towards her bag, where she kept her lock-picking tools.

"Why does Marcus want the Catalyst so badly?" Ethan asked, trying to keep the man talking. "What does he plan to do with it?"

"That's none of your business," the man snapped. "All you need to know is that you're in way over your head. Now, hand it over."

Claire's fingers found the handle of a small tool in her bag. She gave Ethan a barely perceptible nod. Ethan swallowed hard, readying himself.

"Alright," Ethan said, slowly reaching into his bag. "I'll give it to you. Just... don't shoot."

The man's eyes followed Ethan's hand, his attention momentarily diverted. In that split second, Claire sprang into action. She lunged at the man, striking his wrist with the tool and knocking the gun from his hand. The weapon clattered to the ground, and Ethan kicked it away.

The man cursed and swung at Claire, but she dodged, moving with a fluid grace that caught him off guard. Ethan grabbed the laptop and USB drive, his adrenaline spiking as he watched the struggle. Claire landed a solid punch, sending the man stumbling back. But he recovered quickly, pulling a knife from his belt.

"Run!" Claire shouted, keeping her eyes on the man.

Ethan hesitated, torn between fleeing and helping Claire. But Claire's fierce determination left him no choice. He turned and sprinted towards the safe house, the laptop and USB drive clutched tightly in his arms.

Behind him, he heard the sounds of a scuffle, grunts and shouts echoing in the night. He glanced back just in time to see Claire disarm the man, the knife skidding across the pavement. She followed him, her breaths ragged but determined.

They reached the door of the safe house, and Ethan fumbled with the keys, his hands shaking. Claire kept watch, her eyes scanning the shadows for any sign of pursuit. Finally, the door swung open, and they slipped inside, slamming it shut behind them.

Ethan locked the door and leaned against it, his chest heaving. Claire slid down to the floor, her face pale but resolute.

"That was too close," Ethan said, his voice shaking.

Claire nodded, her eyes still sharp and alert. "We need to figure out who else might be after us. Marcus won't stop, and that guy was too skilled to be working alone."

Ethan set the laptop and USB drive on a nearby table, his mind racing. "We have to assume that Marcus has more people on his payroll. We need to secure this place and find out exactly what we're dealing with."

They moved quickly, setting up makeshift barricades and checking the windows. Ethan pulled out his phone and called Cipher, explaining what had happened.

Cipher's voice was tense. "This is worse than I thought. Marcus must have a mole inside Titan Technologies, feeding him information and resources. We need to find out who it is."

Ethan's stomach churned. A corporate spy meant that their enemies were closer than they realized. "How do we do that?"

"I'll start tracing communication patterns and looking for anomalies," Cipher replied. "But it'll take time. You need to stay hidden and keep the Catalyst safe."

Ethan agreed and hung up, turning to Claire. "We need to stay vigilant. Cipher is working on identifying the spy, but until then, we can't let our guard down."

Claire nodded, her expression grim. "Agreed. We also need to think about our next move. We can't just sit here and wait for them to come to us."

Ethan sat down, pulling the laptop towards him. "We have the data from Marcus's laptop. Maybe there's something in here that can help us. A clue, a contact, anything."

They spent the next several hours combing through the files, their exhaustion forgotten in the face of their urgent task. The data was vast and complex, filled with technical schematics, encrypted messages, and corporate documents. As the night wore on, the first light of dawn began to filter through the cracks in the barricades.

Just as they were about to take a break, Claire's eyes widened. "Ethan, look at this."

Ethan leaned over, squinting at the screen. It was an email thread between Marcus and an unidentified contact within Titan Technologies. The messages were heavily coded, but one name stood out—a project codenamed "Pandora."

"Pandora?" Ethan muttered, his mind racing. "What is that?"

Claire's fingers flew over the keyboard, decrypting the messages as quickly as she could. "It looks like a top-secret initiative within Titan Technologies. Marcus has been siphoning resources and information from it to develop his own version of the Catalyst."

Ethan's heart pounded. "We need to expose this. If we can prove that Marcus is stealing from Titan, we can turn the tables on him."

Claire nodded, determination etched into her features. "But first, we need to find the spy and gather solid evidence. This isn't just about the Catalyst anymore. It's about stopping Marcus before he can do any more damage."

They worked in silence, the weight of their mission pressing down on them. As the first rays of sunlight pierced through the darkness, Ethan felt a renewed sense of purpose. They were up against a formidable enemy, but they had each other and the truth on their side.

The hunt for the corporate spy was on, and Ethan knew that every step they took brought them closer to exposing the corruption within Titan Technologies. The stakes had never been higher, and the danger was greater than ever, but they were ready to face whatever came their way.

As they continued their work, a sudden loud bang echoed from the front of the house, followed by the sound of splintering wood. Ethan and Claire exchanged a glance, their eyes wide with fear and determination. The battle was far from over, and their enemies were closing in.

7

The Prototype

The front door splintered under the force of a heavy blow, sending shards of wood flying into the room. Ethan and Claire sprang to their feet, their hearts pounding. The barricades they had hastily erected wouldn't hold for long against such a determined assault.

Ethan grabbed the Catalyst and the laptop, while Claire snatched up the USB drive and her bag of tools. They exchanged a silent nod, then darted towards the back of the house. The sounds of boots stomping on broken wood echoed through the hallway as their pursuers entered.

"This way," Claire whispered, leading Ethan towards a narrow staircase that descended into the basement.

As they hurried down the steps, Ethan could hear the intruders ransacking the ground floor, their voices barking orders to search every inch of the place. The basement was dark and musty, filled with old furniture and forgotten boxes. Claire pulled a heavy shelf across the door, hoping to buy them a few extra minutes.

"We need to get out of here," Ethan said, his voice low and urgent.

Claire nodded, her eyes scanning the room. "There," she pointed to a small window near the ceiling, barely large enough for them to squeeze through.

Ethan handed her the Catalyst and the laptop, then hoisted her up to the window. Claire pushed the window open and wriggled through, dropping to the ground outside. She turned back to help Ethan, who struggled to fit his broad shoulders through the narrow frame.

"Hurry!" Claire urged, glancing nervously at the basement door, which was now shuddering under the force of the intruders' blows.

Ethan gritted his teeth and forced himself through, landing in a heap beside Claire. They sprinted away from the house, their breaths coming in ragged gasps. The first light of dawn was beginning to brighten the sky, casting long shadows across the deserted street.

They didn't stop running until they reached the cover of a nearby alley. There, they crouched behind a dumpster, trying to catch their breath.

"That was too close," Ethan said, wiping sweat from his brow.

Claire nodded, her eyes wide with fear and determination. "We need to find a new place to hide. Somewhere they won't think to look for us."

Ethan glanced around, his mind racing. "I know a place. An old warehouse where I used to work on prototypes. It's been abandoned for years. No one will think to look there."

Claire nodded. "Lead the way."

They moved quickly through the backstreets, keeping to the shadows and avoiding main roads. The warehouse was on the outskirts of town, hidden among a cluster of derelict buildings. They reached it just as the sun was fully rising, bathing the world in a golden light.

The warehouse was a hulking, rusted structure, its windows broken and its doors hanging off their hinges. Ethan pushed open a side door and led Claire inside. The interior was a maze of old machinery and discarded materials, but it provided the cover they needed.

Ethan set up his laptop on a rickety table, and Claire plugged in the USB drive. They had to work quickly, knowing that their pursuers wouldn't give up easily.

"We need to decrypt the rest of these files," Claire said, her fingers flying over the keyboard. "There has to be something in here that we can use against Marcus."

Ethan nodded, his mind already focused on the task. As they worked, the sounds of the outside world faded away, leaving only the hum of the laptop and the clicking of keys.

Hours passed. The sun climbed higher in the sky, its rays filtering through the broken windows and casting patterns of light and shadow across the room. The tension in the air was palpable, but they kept working, driven by a shared determination to bring Marcus down.

Finally, Claire let out a triumphant cry. "I found something!"

Ethan hurried over, his eyes scanning the screen. Claire had decrypted a series of emails between Marcus and an unknown contact within Titan Technologies. The messages detailed the construction of a secret prototype—an advanced version of the Catalyst designed to be weaponized.

"This is it," Ethan said, his voice filled with a mix of dread and resolve. "We have to expose this. If Marcus gets his hands on a weaponized Catalyst, it could be catastrophic."

Claire nodded. "We need to get this to the authorities. But first, we have to secure the prototype. If we can get our hands on it, we'll have concrete evidence to bring Marcus down."

Ethan thought for a moment. "There's an old lab on the outskirts of town. It's where I developed the original Catalyst. If Marcus is building a prototype, it's the perfect place to hide it."

Claire agreed, and they quickly packed up their equipment. As they left the warehouse, Ethan couldn't shake the feeling that they were being watched. Every shadow seemed to hold a hidden threat, every sound a potential danger.

They reached the lab just as dusk was falling. The building was surrounded by a tall, chain-link fence topped with barbed wire. It looked abandoned, but Ethan knew better.

"We need to be careful," he whispered. "If Marcus has people guarding the prototype, we'll have to take them by surprise."

They slipped through a gap in the fence and made their way towards the lab, keeping low to the ground. The windows were dark, but Ethan could see a faint glow coming from the back of the building.

They reached the entrance and carefully pushed the door open. Inside, the lab was eerily quiet, the air thick with dust and the scent of old chemicals. They moved cautiously, their eyes scanning every corner for signs of danger.

As they approached the back of the lab, they heard voices. Ethan motioned for Claire to stay low, and they crept closer, peering around a corner. In the center of the room, surrounded by equipment and blueprints, was the prototype.

It was sleek and advanced, a more refined version of the Catalyst. Two men in lab coats were working on it, their attention focused on the device.

"We need to take them out quietly," Ethan whispered. "We can't let them alert Marcus."

Claire nodded, pulling a small, silenced pistol from her bag. Ethan's eyes widened in surprise, but he didn't question it. They moved in unison, their steps silent on the concrete floor.

Claire took aim and fired, the shots barely making a sound. The men crumpled to the ground, unconscious. Ethan hurried over to the prototype, carefully disconnecting it from the equipment.

"We have it," he said, a sense of triumph in his voice. "Now we need to get out of here."

They made their way back through the lab, the prototype securely in Ethan's hands. As they reached the door, a sudden noise stopped them in their tracks. The sound of footsteps echoed through the hallway, drawing closer.

"We need to move," Claire hissed, her eyes wide with fear.

Ethan nodded, and they bolted for the exit. They burst through the door and into the night, the sounds of pursuit close behind. They sprinted towards the fence, adrenaline giving them speed. Ethan slipped through the gap first, followed closely by Claire.

Just as they cleared the fence, a gunshot rang out. Ethan felt a searing pain in his side, and he stumbled, nearly dropping the prototype. Claire grabbed him, helping him to his feet.

"Keep moving!" she urged, her voice filled with determination.

They ran into the darkness, the sounds of pursuit growing fainter. They didn't stop until they reached a safe distance, their breaths coming in ragged gasps.

Ethan collapsed against a tree, clutching his side. The pain was intense, but he knew they couldn't afford to stop.

"We did it," he gasped, a weak smile on his face. "We have the prototype."

Claire nodded, her eyes filled with determination. "We're not done yet. We need to get this to the authorities and expose Marcus. This is just the beginning."

As they moved through the darkness, Ethan felt a renewed sense of hope. They had the evidence they needed, and with Claire by his side, he knew they could take down Marcus and protect the Catalyst. The battle was far from over, but they were ready to face whatever came next.

8

The Government's Interest

Ethan's vision blurred as Claire drove through the winding roads, his side throbbing with each bump and turn. The gunshot wound wasn't deep, but it was enough to sap his strength. Claire kept glancing at him, her expression tight with worry.

"We need to find help, Ethan. You're losing too much blood."

Ethan shook his head, wincing at the pain. "No hospitals. Marcus has eyes everywhere. We have to keep moving."

Claire nodded, her knuckles white on the steering wheel. "There's a safe house not far from here. We can regroup and figure out our next move."

The safe house was a small cabin hidden deep in the woods, accessible only by a narrow, overgrown path. Claire pulled up and helped Ethan inside, laying him gently on a worn-out couch. She tore open a first aid kit and began cleaning the wound, her hands steady despite the fear in her eyes.

As she worked, Ethan's mind raced. They had the prototype and the data, but they were still far from safe. Marcus wouldn't stop until he had the Catalyst, and now the stakes were higher than ever. Ethan knew they needed more help, someone with the resources to take on a powerful corporation like Titan Technologies.

Suddenly, Claire's phone buzzed. She glanced at the screen, her expression unreadable. "It's Cipher. She's found something."

Claire handed the phone to Ethan, who put it on speaker. Cipher's voice crackled through the line, filled with urgency.

"I've traced the source of the prototype's funding. It's coming from a secret division within the Department of Energy. They've been funneling money and resources to Marcus, likely without official approval."

Ethan's heart sank. "The government's involved?"

"Not officially," Cipher replied. "It's a rogue faction operating under the radar. But this means we have a potential ally. If we can expose this, the legitimate authorities might step in."

Claire finished bandaging Ethan's wound and took the phone. "How do we do that?"

"I've set up a meeting with a contact in the Department of Energy," Cipher said. "He's trustworthy and can help us bring this to light. You need to meet him tonight."

Ethan sat up, gritting his teeth against the pain. "Where?"

Cipher gave them the location: a secluded park on the edge of the city. Claire ended the call and helped Ethan to his feet.

"We need to get moving," she said, her voice firm. "This is our chance."

They drove in silence, the tension thick in the air. Ethan's mind was a whirl of thoughts and fears. If they could convince this contact to help, they might have a shot at stopping Marcus. But if he was compromised, it could be a trap.

They arrived at the park just as the sun was setting, casting long shadows over the empty pathways. Claire parked the car and helped Ethan out. They made their way to a bench near a small pond, the meeting spot Cipher had arranged.

Minutes ticked by, each one feeling like an eternity. Ethan's senses were on high alert, his eyes scanning the area for any sign of danger. Finally, a man approached, his hands in his pockets. He looked around cautiously before sitting down on the bench opposite them.

"You must be Dr. Cole," the man said, his voice low. "I'm Agent Harris. Cipher told me about your situation."

Ethan nodded, wincing as he adjusted his position. "We need your help. Marcus Holloway has developed a weaponized version of the Catalyst. We have the prototype and the evidence, but we can't fight him alone."

Agent Harris's expression was grave. "I know. I've been trying to expose this rogue operation for months. If you have the prototype and the data, we can take this to the higher-ups and shut it down."

Claire handed him the USB drive, her eyes never leaving his face. "This has everything. We need to act fast."

Harris plugged the drive into a secure tablet and began reviewing the files. His face hardened as he read through the encrypted emails and technical schematics. "This is worse than I thought. Marcus isn't just building a weapon—he's planning to sell it to the highest bidder. Terrorists, enemy states, anyone with enough money."

Ethan's blood ran cold. "We have to stop him."

Harris nodded. "I'll get this to my superiors. But we need to move carefully. If Marcus finds out we're onto him, he'll go underground and we'll lose our chance."

Suddenly, a rustling in the bushes caught their attention. Harris's hand went to his sidearm, and Claire stood up, ready to defend them. A figure emerged from the shadows, and Ethan's heart sank as he recognized the man.

It was one of Marcus's enforcers, the same man who had attacked them at the safe house. He smirked, his eyes gleaming with malice.

"Did you really think you could get away from us?" he sneered, pulling out a gun.

Harris reacted instantly, drawing his weapon and firing. The enforcer dropped to the ground, clutching his shoulder, but not before getting off a shot of his own. Claire cried out as the bullet grazed her arm, and Ethan felt a surge of rage and fear.

"We need to go, now!" Harris shouted, helping Claire to her feet.

They ran through the park, Harris covering their retreat. Ethan's side burned with pain, but he pushed through, driven by the urgency of their mission. They reached the car, and Harris got behind the wheel, speeding away as more of Marcus's men appeared in the distance.

"Where are we going?" Ethan asked, his breath coming in ragged gasps.

"To a secure location," Harris replied, his eyes focused on the road. "We'll be safe there, and I'll get the data to my superiors. We're not out of the woods yet, but we have a chance."

Ethan leaned back, clutching the Catalyst tightly. The battle was far from over, but for the first time, they had a glimmer of hope. With Agent Harris on their side, they had a fighting chance to expose Marcus and protect the Catalyst.

As they sped through the night, Ethan couldn't shake the feeling that the stakes were even higher than they realized. The rogue faction within the government, Marcus's plans to sell the weaponized Catalyst—there was so much more at play. But with Claire and Harris by his side, he knew they would fight until the end.

The road ahead was fraught with danger, but they were ready to face whatever came next.

9

The Global Pursuit

The secure location turned out to be a safe house on the outskirts of a quiet suburb. Harris led Ethan and Claire inside, where a small team of agents was already waiting. The atmosphere was tense, the air thick with the urgency of their mission. Ethan and Claire were ushered into a makeshift command center, where Harris immediately began briefing his team.

Ethan's wound had been treated, but he still felt the dull throb of pain as he sat at a table, the Catalyst and laptop before him. Claire hovered nearby, her eyes sharp and alert. Harris approached, holding a map marked with several locations.

"Marcus's network is extensive," Harris began, pointing to various points on the map. "He's got operatives in multiple countries, and he's been using them to gather the components for the weaponized Catalyst. If we're going to stop him, we need to shut down these operations globally."

Ethan felt a surge of determination. "What do we need to do?"

Harris's expression was grim. "We're splitting into teams. We need to hit these locations simultaneously to prevent Marcus from relocating. You'll be going to Germany. There's a facility there where they're developing the final components. Claire, you'll go with him. My team will handle the stateside operations."

Claire nodded, her resolve unwavering. "We're ready."

Harris handed them new identification documents and a dossier with the details of their mission. "You'll be posing as consultants from a tech company. Your contact in Germany will meet you at the airport and provide further instructions. Be careful. Marcus's men will be watching."

The flight to Germany was long and fraught with tension. Ethan and Claire spoke little, each lost in their thoughts. The weight of their mission pressed heavily on them, but they knew there was no turning back.

At the Berlin airport, they were met by their contact, a tall, stern-faced man named Klaus. He led them to a discreet car and drove them to a nondescript building on the outskirts of the city.

"This is our staging area," Klaus explained as they entered. "The facility you need to infiltrate is heavily guarded. We've arranged for you to attend a conference there as representatives of your cover company. Once inside, you'll need to find the main server room and plant this device." He handed Ethan a small, inconspicuous gadget.

"What does it do?" Claire asked, examining the device.

"It will upload a virus to their system, disrupting their operations and allowing us to extract the data we need," Klaus replied. "You'll have a small window of time to get in and out. Once the virus is active, their security will be compromised, but only for a short period."

Ethan and Claire spent the next few hours going over the plan in detail. They memorized the layout of the facility, familiarized themselves with their cover identities, and rehearsed their entry and exit strategies. As night fell, the weight of the mission settled heavily on their shoulders.

The next morning, they arrived at the facility dressed as consultants, their new IDs getting them past the initial security checks. The building was sleek and modern, its corridors bustling with scientists and engineers. Ethan's heart pounded as they made their way to the conference room, the small device hidden in his briefcase.

The conference proceeded smoothly, their cover identities holding up under scrutiny. During a break, Ethan and Claire slipped away, navigating the labyrinthine halls towards the server room. They passed several checkpoints, each one a nerve-wracking encounter, but their forged credentials held up.

Finally, they reached the server room. Ethan took a deep breath and swiped his access card, praying it would work. The door clicked open, and they slipped inside. The room was filled with rows of servers, their lights blinking rhythmically.

"Let's do this quickly," Claire whispered, her eyes darting around for any sign of security.

Ethan found the main terminal and plugged in the device. The screen flickered as the virus uploaded, lines of code streaming past. He kept glancing at the door, expecting guards to burst in at any moment.

Just as the upload completed, an alarm blared. Red lights flashed, and a voice over the intercom announced a security breach. Claire's eyes widened in alarm.

"We need to go, now!" she urged.

They bolted from the server room, the corridors now filled with panicked employees and security personnel. Ethan clutched the laptop and the Catalyst, his heart racing. They navigated the chaos, heading towards the exit, but the path was blocked by guards.

"This way!" Claire shouted, pulling Ethan towards a side corridor.

They sprinted down the narrow hall, the sounds of pursuit growing louder behind them. They burst through a fire exit and into a loading bay, where Klaus was waiting in a van.

"Get in!" he shouted, the engine already running.

Ethan and Claire dove into the back, the van screeching away as guards spilled out of the building, firing shots that pinged off the metal exterior. Ethan winced as a bullet grazed the side of the van, but they sped away, leaving the facility behind.

They didn't relax until they were well out of the city, the adrenaline still coursing through their veins. Klaus drove them to a secluded safe house, where they regrouped and assessed the damage.

"The virus worked," Ethan said, his voice shaky with relief. "We have the data."

Klaus nodded, his expression serious. "Good. We've already disrupted Marcus's operations here. The other teams are reporting similar success. But this isn't over yet. We need to take this data back to Harris and expose Marcus once and for all."

Ethan and Claire exchanged a glance, their resolve unbroken. They had survived the first leg of their global pursuit, but the real battle was still ahead. With the evidence in hand, they were one step closer to stopping Marcus and protecting the Catalyst. The stakes were higher than ever, but they were ready to face whatever came next.

10

The Betrayal

The safe house was eerily quiet, the tension thick in the air. Ethan sat at a table, reviewing the data they had extracted from the German facility. Claire and Klaus were nearby, discussing their next move. The information they had gathered was explosive—proof of Marcus's illegal activities and his plans to sell the weaponized Catalyst to hostile entities.

As they worked, Ethan couldn't shake the feeling that something was off. Klaus had been instrumental in their success, but there was an undercurrent of unease that he couldn't quite place. He glanced at Claire, who seemed equally on edge.

"We need to get this to Harris," Ethan said, breaking the silence. "This data is our ticket to taking Marcus down."

Klaus nodded, but his eyes held a shadow of doubt. "I'll make the arrangements. We should leave as soon as possible."

Ethan watched Klaus walk away, his mind racing. There was something about Klaus's demeanor that bothered him, a subtle shift in his attitude since they had returned. He turned to Claire, lowering his voice.

"Do you trust him?" he asked.

Claire hesitated, her brow furrowing. "I'm not sure. He's been helpful, but... something feels wrong."

Ethan nodded, feeling the same uncertainty. "We need to be careful. Marcus has eyes everywhere, and we can't afford to make a mistake now."

Klaus returned a few minutes later, his expression calm. "We have a flight out tonight. Harris will meet us at a secure location in Washington D.C. We'll hand over the data there."

Ethan's unease deepened. "We should double-check the arrangements. Make sure everything is secure."

Klaus's eyes flickered with annoyance, but he nodded. "Of course. I'll make the calls."

As Klaus stepped outside to make the calls, Ethan turned to Claire. "Something's not right. We need a backup plan."

Claire agreed, and they quickly discussed their options. They couldn't afford to be complacent, not when they were so close to exposing Marcus.

When Klaus returned, Ethan and Claire were ready. They gathered their things and followed Klaus to the car, the tension between them palpable. The drive to the airport was silent, each of them lost in their thoughts.

At the airport, Klaus led them through security, his demeanor professional and unyielding. They boarded a private jet, provided by the Department of Energy, and settled in for the long flight. Ethan couldn't shake the feeling of impending danger, his instincts screaming at him to stay alert.

As the plane ascended, Klaus excused himself to the cockpit, leaving Ethan and Claire alone. Ethan leaned in, his voice barely a whisper.

"Something's off. We need to be ready for anything."

Claire nodded, her eyes scanning the cabin. "Agreed. Let's keep our guard up."

Hours passed, the hum of the engines a constant backdrop to their unease. As they neared their destination, the tension reached a breaking point. Suddenly, the plane lurched, and the lights flickered.

"What's happening?" Claire exclaimed, gripping the armrest.

Ethan's heart raced. "I don't know. Stay ready."

The plane stabilized, but the intercom crackled to life. Klaus's voice echoed through the cabin. "We're experiencing some turbulence. Nothing to worry about."

Ethan's suspicion deepened. He stood and moved towards the cockpit, but the door was locked. He knocked, trying to keep his voice calm. "Klaus, what's going on?"

No response. Claire joined him, her eyes wide with fear. "Ethan, something's wrong."

Suddenly, the cockpit door burst open, and two armed men stormed out, guns trained on Ethan and Claire. Klaus followed, a grim smile on his face.

"I'm sorry, Ethan," Klaus said, his voice cold. "But Marcus made me an offer I couldn't refuse."

Betrayal hit Ethan like a physical blow. "You were working with him all along."

Klaus shrugged. "Not at first. But Marcus has resources. Power. I couldn't pass it up."

Claire's eyes blazed with anger. "You sold us out."

Klaus's smile widened. "It's nothing personal. Just business."

The armed men forced Ethan and Claire back to their seats, their guns never wavering. Klaus sat across from them, his demeanor relaxed.

"You're going to hand over the data," Klaus said. "And then you're going to disappear. Marcus has plans for the Catalyst, and there's nothing you can do to stop him."

Ethan's mind raced, searching for a way out. The plane's confined space offered little room for maneuvering, and the armed men were watching their every move. He glanced at Claire, her face set in determination.

As the plane began its descent, Ethan knew they had to act fast. He leaned in, his voice barely a whisper. "Follow my lead."

Claire gave a subtle nod, her eyes locked on Klaus. Ethan took a deep breath, his mind racing. They needed a distraction, something to throw their captors off balance.

Suddenly, the plane jolted as it hit turbulence. Ethan seized the moment, lunging at the nearest armed man. The surprise move caught the man off guard, and Ethan wrestled the gun from his grip. Claire moved with lightning speed, disarming the second man and aiming the weapon at Klaus.

"Drop it!" she shouted, her voice filled with authority.

Klaus hesitated, his eyes darting between Ethan and Claire. Seeing no way out, he raised his hands in surrender.

Ethan's heart pounded as he secured the gun, keeping it trained on Klaus. "You're going to land this plane, and we're going to walk away. Try anything, and you won't live to see Marcus's plans succeed."

Klaus's face twisted with anger, but he nodded. "Fine. But this isn't over."

Ethan and Claire kept their weapons trained on Klaus and the disarmed men as the plane descended. The tension was palpable, every second stretching into an eternity. Finally, the plane touched down on a secluded airstrip.

They forced Klaus and his men off the plane, securing them with zip ties they found in the cabin. Ethan grabbed the Catalyst and the laptop, his mind focused on the next step.

"We need to get to Harris," Claire said, her voice steady despite the fear in her eyes.

Ethan nodded. "Let's move."

They left Klaus and his men on the tarmac, hurrying towards a waiting vehicle. As they drove away, Ethan felt a mixture of relief and determination. They had survived the betrayal, but the battle was far from over.

With the evidence in hand, they were closer than ever to exposing Marcus and protecting the Catalyst. But as they sped towards their meeting with Harris, Ethan couldn't shake the feeling that the real fight had only just begun. The stakes were higher than ever, and their enemies were closing in. But together, they were ready to face whatever came next.

11

The Final Showdown

Ethan and Claire sped through the darkened streets of Washington D.C., their hearts pounding with the urgency of their mission. The city's lights blurred past as they navigated towards the rendezvous point with Agent Harris. The weight of the Catalyst and the laptop seemed to press down on Ethan's lap like a physical burden, each second ticking by with agonizing slowness.

They arrived at an abandoned warehouse near the waterfront, the meeting place chosen for its seclusion. The building loomed ominously, its windows dark and broken. They parked the car and approached cautiously, their senses heightened by the threat that hung over them.

Ethan knocked on the heavy metal door in a predetermined sequence, and a moment later, it creaked open. Agent Harris stood on the other side, his face tense with urgency.

"Get inside, quickly," Harris urged, scanning the area behind them before closing the door.

Inside, a makeshift command center had been set up. Computers and communication equipment lined the walls, and a small team of agents worked quietly, their faces illuminated by the glow of their screens. Harris led Ethan and Claire to a table at the center of the room.

"We don't have much time," Harris said, his voice low and urgent. "Marcus's network is closing in. We need to move fast."

Ethan placed the laptop and the Catalyst on the table, his hands steady despite the turmoil within him. "We have the evidence. We need to make it public and bring Marcus down."

Harris nodded, his eyes hardening with resolve. "We're already working on it. We've intercepted communications indicating that Marcus is planning something big. We need to stop him before he can put his plan into action."

As they spoke, a loud crash echoed from outside, followed by the sound of gunfire. The agents in the room sprang into action, their training kicking in. Harris grabbed a radio and barked orders, his face a mask of concentration.

"Ethan, Claire, get to cover," Harris ordered, drawing his weapon. "We've been compromised."

Ethan and Claire ducked behind a row of crates, their hearts pounding. The sound of gunfire grew louder, punctuated by the shouts of agents and the thud of boots on concrete. Ethan peeked over the top of the crates, his eyes widening as he saw Marcus's men storming the building.

"We have to protect the Catalyst," Claire whispered, her voice tight with fear and determination.

Ethan nodded, his mind racing. "We can't let them take it. It's our only leverage."

They watched as Harris and his team engaged Marcus's men in a fierce firefight, the air thick with the smell of gunpowder and the acrid taste of fear. Ethan's heart raced as he weighed their options. They needed to get the Catalyst and the data to safety, but the exit was blocked.

Suddenly, an explosion rocked the building, sending debris flying. The shockwave knocked Ethan and Claire off their feet, the noise deafening. Ethan struggled to his feet, his ears ringing. Through the haze of smoke and dust, he saw Harris fighting off two attackers, his face grim with determination.

"Go!" Harris shouted, his voice barely audible over the chaos. "Get the Catalyst out of here!"

Ethan grabbed the Catalyst and the laptop, his mind focused on a single goal: escape. Claire was at his side, her face set in grim resolve. Together, they moved towards a side door, using the chaos as cover.

They slipped through the door and into a narrow alleyway, the sounds of the battle fading behind them. The night air was cold and sharp, a stark contrast to the stifling heat of the warehouse. They ran down the alley, their footsteps echoing off the brick walls.

As they reached the end of the alley, a black SUV screeched to a halt in front of them. The door flew open, and Cipher leaned out, her face etched with urgency.

"Get in!" she shouted.

Ethan and Claire didn't hesitate. They dove into the SUV, and Cipher floored the gas pedal, the tires screeching as they sped away. Ethan clutched the Catalyst and the laptop, his mind reeling from the night's events.

"We need to get this data to the media," Cipher said, her voice tight with determination. "It's the only way to expose Marcus and stop him."

Ethan nodded, his resolve hardening. "Let's do it."

They navigated the dark streets, the tension in the SUV palpable. Cipher drove with practiced precision, her eyes scanning the road for any sign of pursuit. They reached a nondescript office building in the heart of the city, its lights darkened to avoid attracting attention.

"This is a secure communications hub," Cipher explained as they entered the building. "We can upload the data from here and ensure it reaches every major news outlet."

They moved quickly, setting up the laptop and connecting it to the building's secure network. Ethan's hands shook as he typed, the weight of their mission pressing down on him. Claire stood by his side, her presence a steadying force.

"Uploading now," Ethan said, his voice filled with a mix of fear and hope.

The screen flickered as the data transferred, each percentage point feeling like an eternity. Suddenly, the lights flickered, and the building's security alarms blared.

"They've found us," Cipher said, her voice tight with urgency. "We need to hold them off until the upload is complete."

Ethan and Claire grabbed their weapons, positioning themselves near the entrance. The sound of approaching footsteps echoed through the building, growing louder with each passing second.

The door burst open, and Marcus's men stormed in, their guns blazing. Ethan and Claire returned fire, the air filled with the deafening roar of gunfire and the acrid smell of smoke. Cipher worked furiously at the computer, her fingers flying over the keyboard.

"We're almost there!" Cipher shouted over the noise. "Just a little longer!"

Ethan's heart pounded as he fought off the attackers, each moment a desperate struggle for survival. Claire was at his side, her face set in grim determination. They couldn't let Marcus win. Not now. Not when they were so close.

Suddenly, the screen flashed a message: Upload Complete. Cipher let out a triumphant cry, and Ethan felt a surge of relief. But their victory was short-lived. Marcus himself stepped into the room, his eyes cold and furious.

"This ends now," Marcus said, his voice a low growl.

Ethan stood his ground, his weapon trained on Marcus. "It's over, Marcus. The world knows. You've lost."

Marcus's face twisted with rage, and he raised his gun. But before he could fire, Harris burst into the room, his weapon drawn.

"Drop it, Marcus!" Harris shouted. "It's over!"

Marcus hesitated, his eyes flicking between Ethan and Harris. He saw the determination in their faces, the unwavering resolve. Slowly, he lowered his gun, his face a mask of fury.

"You've won this round," Marcus snarled. "But this isn't over."

Harris moved forward, securing Marcus and his remaining men. The tension in the room began to ease, replaced by a sense of cautious relief. Ethan and Claire lowered their weapons, their hearts still racing.

"We did it," Claire said, her voice filled with exhaustion and triumph.

Ethan nodded, feeling the weight of their journey finally lift. "We stopped him."

As the authorities arrived to take Marcus and his men into custody, Ethan felt a sense of peace. The Catalyst was safe, and Marcus's plans had been exposed. The battle was over, but the fight for a better future had just begun.

Together, Ethan and Claire walked out into the dawn, ready to face whatever challenges lay ahead. They had fought for what was right, and in the end, they had won.

12

The New Dawn

The sun was just beginning to rise over Washington D.C., casting a golden glow across the city. Ethan and Claire stood outside the makeshift command center, the weight of their victory still settling in. The air was crisp, the sounds of the city starting to stir. They had done it—Marcus had been arrested, and the Catalyst was safe.

But the fight wasn't over. Ethan knew that the fallout from their actions would ripple through the corridors of power for months, maybe years. The data they had uploaded was already making headlines, exposing the extent of Marcus's corruption and the shadowy network that had supported him. It was a victory, but one that came with its own set of challenges.

Cipher emerged from the building, her face lit by a mixture of relief and determination. "The data's been verified. Every major news outlet is running with the story. Marcus's network is collapsing."

Ethan nodded, the enormity of what they had accomplished beginning to sink in. "What about the rogue faction in the Department of Energy?"

"Already being dismantled," Cipher replied. "Harris's superiors are moving quickly to clean house. The legitimate authorities are on it."

Claire stepped closer, her expression one of both pride and exhaustion. "We did it, Ethan. The Catalyst is safe. The world knows the truth."

Ethan felt a swell of gratitude for his allies—for Claire, for Cipher, for Harris. They had stood by him through the darkest moments, and together they had achieved something monumental. But as he looked around, he realized that their work was far from finished.

"We need to ensure the Catalyst is used for good," Ethan said, his voice steady. "It can't fall into the wrong hands again."

Cipher nodded. "Agreed. We need to establish safeguards, work with trustworthy organizations to develop and distribute it responsibly."

Harris joined them, his face etched with the strain of the last few days but brightened by a hint of a smile. "You did it, Ethan. The Catalyst will change the world, and you've ensured it won't be weaponized."

Ethan took a deep breath, the morning air filling his lungs with a renewed sense of purpose. "We all did it. Now, we have to make sure this change is for the better."

The next few weeks were a whirlwind of activity. Ethan, Claire, and Cipher worked closely with government officials and international organizations to establish a framework for the responsible use of the Catalyst. They formed alliances with scientists, environmentalists, and policymakers, all dedicated to ensuring the technology was used to address global challenges like energy scarcity and climate change.

Ethan found himself speaking at conferences, testifying before committees, and working long hours to lay the groundwork for a new era of innovation and collaboration. The Catalyst had the potential to revolutionize energy consumption, and Ethan was determined to see it used to build a better future.

One evening, as the sun set over the city, Ethan sat in his office, reviewing the latest reports. The door creaked open, and Claire walked in, carrying two cups of coffee. She handed one to Ethan and sat down beside him, her eyes reflecting the same blend of exhaustion and hope that he felt.

"Long day?" Claire asked, a faint smile playing on her lips.

Ethan nodded, taking a sip of the coffee. "But worth it. We're making progress. The Catalyst is being integrated into sustainable energy projects worldwide. It's starting to make a real difference."

Claire leaned back in her chair, her gaze thoughtful. "You know, when we started this journey, I never imagined we'd come this far. We were just trying to protect your invention. Now, we're part of something much bigger."

Ethan reached out and took her hand, his heart filled with gratitude. "I couldn't have done it without you. Without all of you. This is our victory."

Claire squeezed his hand, her eyes shining with determination. "And it's just the beginning. There's so much more to do."

As they sat together, the city lights twinkling outside the window, Ethan felt a sense of peace. They had faced unimaginable dangers, uncovered vast conspiracies, and emerged victorious. But more than that, they had forged a path towards a brighter future.

The Catalyst was more than just a technological breakthrough—it was a symbol of what was possible when people came together for a common cause. It represented hope, innovation, and the power of human ingenuity. And as long as they continued to work together, Ethan knew they could overcome any challenge that lay ahead.

The night wore on, but neither of them moved. They talked about the future, about their dreams and aspirations, and about the world they hoped to build. The bond between them had been forged in the crucible of adversity, and it was stronger than ever.

Eventually, as the first light of dawn began to break, Claire stood and stretched. "We should get some rest. Tomorrow is another big day."

Ethan nodded, feeling a sense of contentment he hadn't known in a long time. "You're right. But tonight, we celebrate. We've earned it."

They left the office together, stepping out into the cool morning air. The city was waking up, the streets beginning to fill with the hum of activity. As they walked, Ethan felt a profound sense of connection to the world around him. They had fought for this moment, and now they had the chance to shape the future.

Hand in hand, they walked towards a new day, ready to face whatever challenges lay ahead. The journey had been long and arduous, but it had also been filled with moments of courage, determination, and hope. And as the sun rose on this new dawn, Ethan knew that they had only just begun to write the next chapter of their story.